HEART & HANDS TAROT

By Liz Blackbird

Copyright © 2021 U.S. Games Systems, Inc.

All rights reserved. The illustrations, cover design, and contents are protected by copyright. No part of this booklet may be reproduced in any form without permission in writing from the publisher, except by a reviewer who wishes to quote brief passages in connection with a review written for inclusion in a magazine, newspaper or website.

10 9 8 7 6 5 4 3

Made in China

Published by
U.S. GAMES SYSTEMS, INC.
179 Ludlow Street
Stamford, CT 06902 USA
www.usgamesinc.com

INTRODUCTION

In a reading, the Fool represents both the beginning of a journey and the enlightened return home. I began this project with the Fool's ambition, crafting the mysterious and powerful Major Arcana cards in my early twenties during a period when I was at my least enlightened, but also at my most confident and attuned with my own creativity. I drew the court cards as I graduated from college and set out to travel and learn about the world. As I experienced my first love, I drew the Cups, and I worked on the Pentacles as I adapted to the responsibilities of my first full-time job. When my relationship ended, I distracted myself by drawing Swords piercing hearts and hands. As a new relationship blossomed and I transitioned to a career with more room for self-expression, I drew the Wands, and felt the fires of neglected creativity and confidence rise within me.

Throughout the years, working on these cards nourished my spirit and kept me rooted in a creative practice even as the distractions and necessities of life vied for precedence. I completed the deck as I turned 30, and entered that decade feeling reborn. I hope that this deck will aid all who use it to look inward and reconnect with their own creativity, confidence, and love.

THE MAJOR ARCANA

0. THE FOOL

A figure walks a road lined with flowers, accompanied by a joyful dog. They set off on this journey oblivious to its hardships; eyes blocked with blossoms, they see only beauty. As the dog trusts the Fool to guide it and care for it, the Fool trusts the road to lead them where they need to go. The Fool's optimism may seem naive, but naiveté can be a kind of wisdom; sometimes enlightenment requires unlearning. A hero's journey ends where it began, and the road in this image loops back on itself, suggesting that these travelers may already possess what they seek. This card indicates that a journey is beginning, and it's time to take a leap. Your perspective is fresh and your passion is keen. You have within you what you need to find your way; don't be discouraged by setbacks or derailed by others' influence. Trust your instincts and follow your heart.

Reversed: You're playing it safe and holding yourself back. You may be afraid of what others think, or you may not trust yourself. Perhaps you don't feel ready to take that first step; there's always more to learn or do to prepare. But you won't progress until you hit the road.

1. THE MAGICIAN

Though the Magician's tricks seem spontaneous, his sleight-of-hand conceals the cleverness behind them. The Magician holds all the aces, and has a few more up his sleeve. He is an artist; he wields a palette and brushes, and a canvas behind him awaits his inspiration. He has mastered the tools of his trade and deploys them with skill and creativity. The Magician has the power to make the ordinary extraordinary, and the charisma to make you believe in him. This card suggests that you have the intelligence, ingenuity and talent required to accomplish your goals. You're well trained and well equipped, and your confidence sets you up for success. Your skill is compelling; don't misuse it.

Reversed: You don't have a clear sense of your own abilities. You may not be as skilled as you think you are, or you may lack confidence in your true talents. This can undermine your endeavors and cause you to mislead those around you, whether you mean to or not. An impartial assessment may help you recalibrate.

2. THE HIGH PRIESTESS

A priestess stands in a yonic mandorla, a crescent moon at her feet. Her hands are clasped reverently, wrapped in a string of prayer beads. While her flowing hair obscures her eyes, a third eye opens above them, showing that her insights rise from inner vision. Her garments swirl in circles that dissolve into the flowers around her, as her meditation connects her to the cycles of nature. This card suggests that feminine wisdom is present. Insights arise from intuition, emotional intelligence, and a respect for the rhythms of nature and of one's own body. The High Priestess perceives that which is invisible to others and can provide transformative shifts in perspective. She may not always be able to explain how she knows what she knows, but her guidance is trustworthy.

Reversed: Emotions and gut feelings lead you astray. Your intuition may be distorted by unprocessed trauma, internalized misogyny, or experiences, activities or individuals that estrange you from your body, your feelings or your natural rhythms. Solitude and soul-searching may be necessary to reconnect with your deeper self.

3. THE EMPRESS

A regal woman radiates confidence and calm. Her body is blooming, and she is proud of its beauty, its bounty and its strength. The Empress uses her authority and charm to create harmony all around her. She enriches, propagates and nurtures. She cultivates relationships and sees things to fruition. As a maternal figure, her power grows from love and creativity. This card suggests that beauty, abundance and wealth are possible for you, but require loving cultivation. Nurturing harmonious relationships will be the first step toward creating the life you want.

Reversed: Your environment is going to seed, possibly due to lack of care. You may be conserving your emotional energies or insulating yourselves from others, stunting your personal growth. This card may also indicate rejection of a caregiver role, or maternal pressure to grow in a direction that feels unnatural.

4. THE EMPEROR

The Emperor stands firmly before an iron fence, his hair and beard curled like a ram's horns. The Emperor sets boundaries and defends his sphere of influence. He creates order and stability in his environment by establishing rules and hierarchies. As a leader and patriarch, the Emperor initiates projects, takes responsibility, and governs with reason and fairness. This card suggests you take charge of your situation. Define the problem and organize your thoughts; your knowledge, expertise and analysis will reveal the best course of action. This card may also represent the protection of a paternal authority figure, or the act of setting and enforcing strong boundaries.

Reversed: Attempts at control are disorganized and ineffectual. You are not applying your energies wisely. You may seek to dominate rather than to lead, or you may cede too much power to repressive authorities. This card may also represent a rejection of hierarchy or traditional masculinity.

5. THE HIEROPHANT

The Hierophant leads a placid bull, raising his hand in benediction. Though the animal is restrained, the blooms on its body suggest beauty and growth. The Hierophant is a scholar and religious leader whose authority is rooted in tradition and institutions. Though his knowledge may be arcane and his thinking rigid, he commands wisdom that has withstood the test of time. This card suggests that established institutions or faith traditions have something to offer you. Appealing to experts may spur your development or help you avoid reinventing the wheel. Laws, traditions and taboos often exist for good reasons, and now may not be the time to break them. Despite his conservatism, the Hierophant holds knowledge that can shift your perspective.

Reversed: Question authority and received dogmas. Attachment to institutions or outdated ways of thinking may hold you back. Discarding false idols may be necessary for growth. This card may also represent disillusionment with authority figures or an inability to conform to external norms, ethics or customs.

6. THE LOVERS

Two androgynous figures are entwined in an embrace, bodies perfectly aligned. The eyes of one have slipped closed, while the other points the way forward. The bold patterns on their bodies suggest the balancing of binaries. The Lovers attract and influence each other, undoing inhibitions and encouraging self-love. Their union is absorbing, transformative and selfless.

This card suggests that there's someone you connect with—romantically, spiritually or otherwise. This connection influences your behavior and your sense of self; you may long to become this person as much as you long to be with them. With honesty and clear communication, this union will bring harmony, self-knowledge, affection and support.

Reversed: Your connection with a significant other unravels, or circumstances pull you apart. Poor boundaries lead you to seek connection in unhealthy ways, or unhealthy emotional patterns turn intimate relationships toxic. Self-care and space may be best right now.

7. THE CHARIOT

A girl races forward on a winding road, winged like the goddess of victory. The flowers in her hair evoke her optimism, and the sunglasses that shield her eyes suggest a cool, protective front. Her hand grips the steering wheel, and her confident smile shows that she knows where she's going. She is driven, and her chariot will take her wherever she wills. This card suggests that you're making a move; maybe toward a career goal, or maybe just in search of a change of scenery. Whatever the case, you're set up for success. Your drive and ambition reduce obstacles to speedbumps. Stay motivated and keep your eyes on the road; the only person who can stop you is yourself!

Reversed: Obstacles and setbacks throw you off course. Small failures may bruise your ego, sap your motivation or cause you to charge forward with ill-conceived backup plans. Check yourself, patch things up and map out your next move.

8. JUSTICE

An androgynous figure balances a scale, eyes obscured. Though they stand solidly, their body maintains equilibrium with constant subtle adjustments, and their nudity discloses every move. Actions have consequences and energies expended in one area may destabilize another. Justice corrects for each change and ensures that we reap what we sow. This card indicates that justice will be served. Instabilities or volatilities may soon be resolved, and someone may receive their reward (or comeuppance). This card can also refer to weighing options, maintaining neutrality or attempting a "balancing act." Be mindful of how your actions could affect others' equilibrium and peace.

Reversed: The situation is not fair. Someone may avoid accountability and punishment, or reward may be meted out based on bias rather than merit. Alternatively, you may misprioritize or overextend yourself. Try to regard your situation impartially; a correction is necessary.

9. THE HERMIT

A Hermit meditates at the base of a tree. His bare skull is the still center around which the beauty of the world spins and radiates. His clothes are simple, and he is alone; his search for truth requires introspection and solitude. The Hermit quietly defines his own path and follows it until he finds what he seeks. This card suggests that soul-searching and self-examination are in order. The truths you seek are within, but finding them may require a change of scenery. Withdrawal from the distractions of everyday life may help you focus your thoughts and gain insight.

Reversed: Lack of self-awareness and distorted perceptions cause feelings of loneliness or abandonment, or drive you to isolation or escapism. You may refuse to face reality, for fear of what you might learn. To resolve this, you may need to seek others' help. But don't fear being alone with your thoughts; self-reflection is a step toward liberation.

10. THE WHEEL OF FORTUNE

An ornate wheel is emblazoned with the phases of the moon, and a skull turns at its center. Eyes swirl around it—some starry, some weeping. Like the moon, the Wheel of Fortune spins and changes, cycling through phases of darkness and illumination. Though the Wheel's turns may be unpredictable, twists of fate are certain. This card suggests that fortune has dropped an opportunity into your lap. Chance events or encounters may bring blessings if you are open to their potential. Unexpected setbacks may have bright sides, and seemingly random events may reveal greater significance. Be adaptable, and don't take anything for granted.

Reversed: Misfortune is in store, through no fault of your own. There's not much you can do but accept this turnabout and make the best of it. The situation will turn around before long.

11. STRENGTH

A woman holds closed the mouth of a lion, who submits calmly to her efforts. The woman's teeth are feline, and her hair mingles with the lion's mane, revealing her affinity to the beast she has tamed. Though her act is courageous, her gaze displays patience and compassion because her strength is rooted in love. This card advises you not to fear your own power; instead, learn to harness it. Base instincts and destructive impulses can be controlled and channeled to accomplish your desires, but only if you accept them for what they are. You are resilient enough to withstand whatever threatens you.

Reversed: You're struggling with your instincts in unproductive ways. Shame may cause you to resist your desires, or you may allow your passions to run rampant, harming those around you. Though repression and dominance may feel like strength, they are rooted in fear. Confront the beast within.

12. THE HANGED MAN

An inverted figure hangs from a branch, its body cocooned in silk. His discarded skin drifts behind him, his face frozen in horror and shock. The caterpillar doesn't know what will happen when it submits to the stasis of the chrysalis; all it knows is that its life could not continue as it was. The Hanged Man may seem stuck, but surrendering control can be the first step toward change. This card suggests that it's time to let go. Inaction can be as important as action, and healing, growth and transformation may simply require time. Releasing old attachments and identities can leave you feeling unmoored, but sometimes drifting for a bit is the only way to land somewhere truly new.

Reversed: Your growth is stagnating. Perhaps you identify too closely with patterns of thought or behavior that no longer serve you. Or perhaps you micromanage your development, convinced that your intelligence or industriousness can bring about the change you seek. But the habits that brought you this far can't take you any further. Admitting you don't have all the answers will be the first step toward finding them.

13. DEATH

A moth emerges from its cocoon, a skull emblazoned on its back. Its old life has ended, and a new one has begun. Released from its limbo, it leaps from its branch to soar toward the moon on new wings. Everything is impermanent; even death. This card suggests that something important is ending. Change can be painful, but it can also bring release. Everything has its season, and the decay of old growth prepares the soil for future harvests. Even the most annihilating loss can elevate your consciousness and spur you to new heights.

Reversed: Something you are struggling to hold onto has already been lost. Living in denial, cursing fate or succumbing to depression will only prolong your suffering and delay the transformation in store for you. There is nothing to fear.

14. TEMPERANCE

A centaur rests in a field of flowers between divergent roads. His cup overflows, and he tips wine back into its bottle. The wheel behind his head recalls the balance maintained by Justice and suggests Temperance's imperative to find a middle path. This card suggests that patience, moderation and self-control are called for. Pleasure is not the same as self-care, but neither is asceticism. Finding your equilibrium and managing your resources wisely will keep you at peak strength. The middle path is often the most sustainable.

Reversed: Your behavior is extreme. You may overindulge, or waste effort resisting harmless desires. Perhaps you sleep all day or exhaust yourself with work. Whatever the case, you're expending your energies inefficiently, and you're not replenishing your reserves. You can't go on like this forever.

15. THE DEVIL

Two nude figures are enclosed by bat-like wings, arms fixed overhead by an unseen captor. Their hair flows sensuously over their faces, preventing them from seeing the nature of their trap. The Devil deceives through seduction; he baits his prey with small pleasures and binds them in cages of their own making. This card suggests that materialism, escapism or hedonism may dominate your thinking, locking you into unproductive patterns. Your mind may be clouded by egotism or self-loathing, or transfixed by external distractions. Look within to discover how you've been snared; you may be your own worst enemy.

Reversed: You know your situation is unhealthy and you're taking steps to change it. An eye-opening experience may have changed your perspective, or the pleasures that intoxicated you may no longer provide the same rush. Though you may still feel trapped, there is a path to freedom.

16. THE TOWER

A bolt from above shatters a high-rise tower; the sturdy edifice collapses in a flash. Bodies rain from it like tears; the tower's residents could not have foreseen this disaster. Diligent work, well-laid plans, entire lives are destroyed, and those who rebuild will start from zero. But somehow, life continues. When the Tower falls, its shadow lifts and new light enters. This card suggests that you are experiencing a shock. A sudden revelation may throw your whole life into question, or a disaster may negate past achievements. Things that seemed stable are collapsing, and the best thing to do is to let them. A fresh start can be a gift, and tragedy can be a teacher. Consider this a wake-up call.

Reversed: This upheaval may not quite rise to the level of crisis—or perhaps you are unwilling to admit that it does. You may cling to the status quo, even as its pillars crumble around you. While this setback could have been worse, returning to business as usual will invite further chaos. A fresh perspective is required.

17. THE STAR

A woman gazes blissfully at the star blooming from her forehead. Her hair flows like water over her shoulders, cleansing and rejuvenating her spirit. The Star is a visionary who understands her place in the cosmos and has faith in the light that guides her. She is dazzled by the brightness and beauty of the universe, and brims with inspiration and enlightenment. This card suggests that a sudden insight may reveal a vision for your future or clarify your calling. You're feeling inspired, and you know your own worth. Trust your inner light; it will show you the way forward.

Reversed: You've become disconnected from the things that inspire you. False perceptions or low confidence undermine your inner compass and prevent you from seeing the big picture. Lacking direction, you apply yourself haphazardly to projects that disappoint. Meditation and introspection may illuminate the way forward.

18. THE MOON

A sleeping woman drifts in a boat without oars, lost in her own dreams. Fish leap from the dark water, revealing flashes of a secret, submerged world. The Moon's mysterious gravity shifts tides and alters her course, whether or not she is aware of its pull. Dazzled by the Moon's strange light, the surrounding eyes are swirled by spirals, suggesting delusion or deception. This card indicates that you're traveling unknown territory. You may not be aware of the forces at play or the dangers around (or within) you. Behavior and emotions—yours and others'—may seem erratic or irrational. Be cautious and look beneath the surface; your instincts and intuitions reveal something important, but they may not mean what you think they do.

Reversed: Shadows lift and things start to make sense. Secrets come to light, delusions are unmasked, traumas are revealed, emotional instabilities are recognized and acknowledged. Alternatively, mysterious forces may influence you, but you may rationalize what's happening, refusing to accept the limits of your understanding. There's more beneath the surface than you imagine; don't ignore it.

19. THE SUN

A radiant sun pours light onto the land, nourishing flowers and rejuvenating the earth. The Sun's face is split like the first division of an embryo, because its light is life giving and revitalizing. Even the buried skeleton is smiling, delighted that the cycle of life continues.

This card indicates that life is good; happiness is all around you. Something you'd hoped for is finally attained, or a cloud that has followed you finally lifts. You feel radiant, refreshed, affirmed and optimistic. This card may also represent a birth or a spiritual rebirth. You may feel like a child again, or like you've been given a new lease on life.

Reversed: You may not adequately appreciate your good fortune. Perhaps you take it for granted, or maybe things simply feel too good to be true (or to last). Circumstances in this case may be slightly less sunny than in the upright position, but you still have many blessings to count.

20. JUDGEMENT

Three figures rise from yonic pods to answer the call of an unearthly eye. Their bodies are deathly thin, but their heads burst into vibrant blossoms, and lush leaves unfurl from their feet. Judgement shocks dead things back to life; its reckoning liberates and revitalizes. This card suggests that something is calling to you; a new phase of life is beginning. An epiphany or revelation may have "blown your mind," awakened you to a new reality, or majorly shifted your paradigm. Now may be the time for a personal reckoning; atoning for past errors and settling accounts will allow you to move forward unencumbered.

Reversed: You're refusing a call; perhaps you distrust the messenger, or perhaps you fear change. Poor judgement or self-doubt may lead you to dismiss the message as irrelevant, or its implications may be too threatening to acknowledge. Don't miss this chance; open yourself to new perspectives.

21. THE WORLD

An androgynous figure sits at the center of a cosmic egg, radiating confidence and calm. A cycle is complete; they have achieved a sense of wholeness. They recognize their own perfection, and this awareness brings abundance. Upon the planetary circle that surrounds them, air and fire swirl, and flowers bloom among strings of pearls. The World contains multitudes; it is self-nourishing and homeostatic. This card indicates that you are coming into your own. A life cycle or major effort reaches culmination and brings you to the peak of your powers. The fruits of your labors sustain you in every way. Celebrate yourself!

Reversed: A life-defining effort is reaching completion, but you're having trouble accepting it. A sense of emptiness may accompany your achievements, and anxiety about what comes next may prevent you from celebrating. Resist inertia and hesitation and trust that you deserve the abundance in store.

THE MINOR ARCANA

ACE OF CUPS

A raised glass overflows; wine, fruits and flowers spill into the hand around it. This card suggests that you are experiencing an abundance of happiness and love. Aces indicate beginnings, so this card may represent birth or conception, a declaration of affection, or an opportunity to follow your passion. Whatever the case, sharing your joy with those around you will only increase it, reinforcing connection and communion.

Reversed: The love you feel or once felt begins to drain you; you may feel empty or hungover. An infatuation gives way to reality, or an unrequited love or unrealizable dream consumes you. Alternatively, you may reject new friendships or hide growing feelings. Connection may bring pain as well as joy.

TWO OF CUPS

Two figures drink from each other's cups. The

cups are full, and the figures' fingers are intimately entwined. This card indicates a passionate, intimate relationship. Two people unite, reconcile, form a partnership or collaborate closely on a meaningful endeavor. Attachments are strong, hearts are in alignment and destinies are linked. Harmony is possible.

Reversed: Problems occur in an intimate relationship. Miscommunication, mismatched desire, power imbalances, distance or other discords inhibit or erode love and connection. These can be resolved, but must be addressed directly and empathically.

THREE OF CUPS

Three figures raise champagne flutes in a toast as a guitarist performs in the background. The table is laden with fruit. This card indicates that a celebration is in order. Creative collaborations and connections bear fruit. You may enter a creative community, attend performances or openings, participate in ritual gatherings, or otherwise bond in festive ways with groups who energize your spirit. Rejoice and be inspired!

Reversed: Celebrations may drain your creative energy rather than replenish it. Certain pleasures or social groups may no longer fulfill you, or your creative projects may stall. Alternatively, you may feel excluded from a group, abandoned by support networks or undermined by friends. It may be time to reprioritize.

FOUR OF CUPS

A figure wrings their hands anxiously. They have drained three cups but remain at the table. A fourth cup is offered. Will it delight or disappoint? This card suggests that you are unsatisfied with your current situation, but unsure what to do next. A period of pleasure and excitement has fizzled and left you unfulfilled. Disillusionment and rumination lead to second-guessing and skepticism about new relationships and opportunities. Mindful meditation would support better decision-making.

Reversed: New relationships or opportunities arise that help you overcome alienation or escape unproductive ruts. Restlessness leads you to throw yourself into new situations or fantasies. Upheavals can stir up old anxieties, but change is ultimately for the best.

FIVE OF CUPS

Beyond a doorway, three cups lay spilled.

Droplets like tears rain from the walls, and the doorframe's long shadow obscures a portrait over the hearth. An upset has occurred and grief is present. But two cups are still full and a bowl of fruit awaits on the table. This card suggests that all is not lost, despite disappointment and regret. Pessimism and self-pity may prevent you from seeing the bigger picture. Consolation is available if you'll accept it.

Reversed: Recovery brings unexpected blessings. Relationships grow stronger; new connections are made. Alternatively, you may merely pretend to move on, projecting a strong front while continuing to suffer. Resist the urge to pick at old wounds.

SIX OF CUPS

Five cups are arrayed by a turntable, and the sixth is captured in a photograph held by tender hands. Spring flowers appear in the photo and weave between the cups' stems. This card suggests that memory can be a comfort, even as seasons change. Fond recollections may color your feelings about the present. Cherish past happiness; reminiscing can inspire hope and optimism.

Reversed: Nostalgia may be counterproductive. Living in the past may be appealing, but it inhibits your ability to act in the present to bring about future happiness. Move on and don't look back.

SEVEN OF CUPS

Seven cups emerge from swirling mist, stuffed with symbols of wealth, domesticity, love, bondage, success, the subconscious and the unknown. Two hands reach toward them, but grasp nothing. This card suggests that your imagination is running wild. Possibilities abound, but daydreams may prevent action. Some of your visions may be pipe dreams, but you're having trouble distinguishing fantasy from reality. Prioritization and decision-making are difficult. Careful reflection is required.

Reversed: Illusions are dispelling, and you've begun to prioritize and take steps to realize your desires. But it's possible to be too decisive. Don't seize on an idea arbitrarily, simply to settle a question; be sure to weigh all the options.

EIGHT OF CUPS

Eight full cups are stacked in the foreground, but hands reach past them, toward the moon. Its face is bright, but it displays death's head.

The road in the background winds forward endlessly. This card suggests that success has been achieved, but it may not feel like enough. Doubt or lack of confidence may prevent you from recognizing your accomplishments, or you may dismiss them as inferior to others'. You may lose interest in projects as soon as you make headway, or seek to flee your situation. Believe in yourself and stay the course.

Reversed: Reminding yourself of what you've achieved brings satisfaction and contentment. Recognizing how far you've come helps you go the final mile. This card may also indicate a homecoming or satisfaction after striving.

NINE OF CUPS

Eight guests hold full cups over a table graced with flowers as the host pours the last glass. The host is proud of all they have accomplished, but they know to serve their guests first. This card suggests that things are turning out as you had hoped, and your efforts produce satisfaction, abundance and prosperity. You want for nothing, and your achievements bring harmony to your environment and relationships. Enjoy your success, but don't rest on your laurels.

Reversed: Success leads to self-satisfaction and

complacency. You may overlook or ignore problems that threaten the value of your accomplishments. You may downplay the contributions of others or avoid accountability for errors. Don't let success go to your head, and don't forget those who helped you along the way!

TEN OF CUPS

Hands clasp each other around a table laden with cups. The cups are full, and the hands weave around them harmoniously, forming a heart. This card suggests that you are surrounded by peace, harmony and a sense of well-being, especially in your home or intimate relationships. Your environment is welcoming and nurturing. You've found your community and feel blessed.

Reversed: Relationships are strained, and a place that felt like home no longer does. Security and happiness disappear, and people go their separate ways. This card may indicate the breakup of a household, "empty nest" syndrome or a stressful move—especially from a place of fond memories.

PRINCESS OF CUPS

A young woman sits at a café table, sipping

coffee and scribbling in a notebook. Her gaze is dreamy, and her fish earrings suggest her ability to navigate the waters of emotion. This card may represent a studious, sensitive, empathic youth—usually feminine, often a poet, writer or artist. This person is loyal, trustworthy and a good listener. She may have a message for you, or the ability to help with plans or projects. This card may also represent creativity, inspiration, contemplation or learning new skills—especially in the arts.

Reversed: A creative and sympathetic but somewhat oversensitive person. She may be a romantic, easily influenced by emotional appeals or idealistic rhetoric. Alternatively, heartaches or traumas may cause her to construct a façade of indifference or cynicism. This card may also represent heartache more generally, or the influence of flattery, seduction or emotional manipulations.

PRINCE OF CUPS

A young man peers shyly over glasses, holding a flower-shaped cup. The lenses of his glasses are emblazoned with blossoms, suggesting his idealism, and a guitar is strapped to his back. The Prince of Cups is a troubadour, seeking and celebrating love. This card may represent a romantic adventurer, usually masculine, with a caring and poetic nature. This person is inspiring, gallant, attractive and gregarious. He introduces you to new people or experiences. Though his intentions are good, his idealism may impair his judgement. This card may also refer to winning another's affections, making grand gestures or expressing deep emotions.

Reversed: Despite his charm, this person is not emotionally honest. He hides his true feelings behind a disaffected mask or revels in showy displays of emotion. He may be unstable, unavailable, and narcissistic or more in love with the idea of love than with any person in particular. This card may also indicate promiscuity, infidelity, or illicit or stigmatized love affairs.

QUEEN OF CUPS

A woman cradles a cup in her arms. Her eyes slip gently closed, and the hearts in her hair show her love overflowing. This card may represent a caring, trustworthy advisor, usually feminine, who soothes insecurities and nurtures emotional growth. This person is intuitive and compassionate, with deep emotional intelligence and a receptive, accommodating nature. This card could also refer to a supportive environment, emotional security or unconditional love.

Reversed: A person whose selflessness and people-pleasing nature cause her to lose touch with her own feelings. She is absorbed by others, which weakens her ability to provide guidance and support. This card could also represent abandonment issues, emotional insecurity or codependency.

KING OF CUPS

A man with kind eyes holds out a large cup. Inside, a lotus blooms, representing wisdom rising from the waters of emotion. His flowing hair suggests feeling, and the braids binding it show that he knows how to harness his emotions. This card may represent an authoritative and emotionally intelligent person, usually masculine, who is dependable and even-keeled. This person has great emotional depth but maintains a placid surface. His advice is informed by empathy and a profound understanding of the human condition. This card could also represent integrity, justice, fairness or the control of one's feelings.

Reversed: A volatile, moody or emotionally manipulative person, usually in a position of authority. He may use his awareness of others' feelings to bully or mislead. Alternatively, he may be self-absorbed and more interested in examining the nuances of his own inner life than in connecting with others. This card could also refer to corruption, duplicity or sentimentality.

ACE OF PENTACLES

A hand holding a pentacle descends toward the earth. The pentacle sprouts like a seedling and the earth opens to welcome it. This card indicates that a seed has been planted and new growth is imminent. A new enterprise, opportunity or windfall will increase your prosperity, security or material comfort. Projects undertaken now will meet with success. Hard work is required, but your efforts will bring satisfaction.

Reversed: Opportunities for material success abound, but you may pursue them too greedily. A focus on accumulation may undermine satisfaction. Alternatively, you may fail to take advantage of these opportunities—you may lack motivation, doubt that success is possible or worry that increased wealth will bring unwanted complications. Prudent and patient cultivation is called for.

TWO OF PENTACLES

Hands juggle pentacles, enclosed by an infinite loop. Fruits, pearls and flowers swirl around one, while raindrops fall toward the other. This card suggests you are balancing multiple obligations or opportunities. You may multitask, take on multiple roles or seek a work-life balance. Alternatively, you may actively manage resources to get the most out of investments, or juggle finances to make ends meet. Whatever the case, you're keeping the balls in the air.

Reversed: Failure to strike or maintain balance will result in financial stress or setbacks. Over-commitment may cause important tasks to drop off your radar—especially those related to communication, documentation or paperwork. You may devote more time and effort to keeping up appearances than to preventing or resolving problems. Managing resources too actively might be counterproductive.

THREE OF PENTACLES

A student employs a compass to draw a perfect pentacle. The model the student hopes to replicate gleams above their desk, dangling from the fingers of a teacher. Earlier efforts are scattered nearby, showing that the student is improving. This card suggests that diligent work in a field that suits your talents will lead to mastery. You are putting in the effort and beginning to see results. A mentor may be available to help you improve or you may seek formal training. Continuing your work in this area will bring rewards.

Reversed: You're not living up to your potential. You may not apply yourself fully, or you may fail to put in the work to develop your skills. You may have difficulty identifying your talents or finding a field you love; or you may fail to find training or employment within that chosen field. Alternatively, you may work hard at something you're not very well suited for. To improve, you'll need to redirect your efforts.

FOUR OF PENTACLES

Four pentacles are clutched like coins in hands heavy with jeweled bangles. In the background, a sturdy brick house stands among trees full of fruit. This card indicates that there is stability and material security in your life. Your resources are well managed, your environment is secure and your investments protect what you've accumulated. Sometimes, this success brings fear—you may worry about being "ripped off" or losing what you've gained. Consequently, this card can also suggest miserliness, hoarding, risk-aversion or conservatism. Even if things feel precarious, trust that you are on stable ground.

Reversed: Your material resources are not secure—impracticality and risk-taking may lead to losses; speculative investments may depreciate; payments may be missed, contested or blocked; or expected returns may be derailed, reduced or delayed. Though this situation is stressful, it is also an opportunity to free yourself from obligations that drain resources, cause volatility or fail to satisfy.

FIVE OF PENTACLES

A thief's knife surreptitiously slits a purse, spilling five pentacles. Clouds gather in the background, blotting out the brilliant sun. This card may indicate that you are experiencing financial or material difficulties, or problems with health or fertility. Whatever the case, the circumstances are beyond your control. But don't be discouraged; this loss is not as insurmountable as it may seem.

Reversed: A period of material or physical hardship comes to an end. This hardship may have been brought about at least in part by immoderate behavior or mismanagement of resources, so reversing it may require a change in mindset.

SIX OF PENTACLES

A hand descends from above, fingers held in a gesture of blessing. It drops three coins into outstretched palms but reserves three more for itself. In the background, towering trees are heavy with fruit. This card suggests that there is abundance and prosperity in your life. This good fortune likely results from social investments. Relationships with benefactors or patrons may bear fruit, and gifts, grants or other financial assistance may be offered to you (or by you). Either way, compassion and generosity are wise investments at this time.

Reversed: Charity and support should be offered without strings; gifts are unlikely to be repaid. Don't give more than you can afford to lose, and consider the impact that unpaid debts or unreciprocated help may have on relationships before offering. This card may also suggest difficulty in receiving aid.

SEVEN OF PENTACLES

Against a background of abundant vines, hands heft a basket of harvested grapes. The bunch lifted for inspection is shining and unblemished. This card suggests that hard work and patient effort will bear fruit. Investments or projects have already begun to show returns, but further time and cultivation will bring even greater rewards. The seeds have been sown, but growth can't be rushed.

Reversed: Diligent effort fails to produce the desired results. Complications derail projects or drain profits. Hasty or impulsive decisions cause setbacks, and impatience or anxiety leads to prioritizing short-term gains over long-term success. Alternatively, the costs of success may outweigh its benefits. You may need to work smarter, rather than harder.

EIGHT OF PENTACLES

Hands polish a newly finished pentacle as examples of past creations gleam in the background. The work desk below is stacked with blanks waiting to be carved. This card suggests that you've identified and developed the abilities necessary to achieve your goals; now you must apply them. The repetitive work required to hone a skill, meet a quota, research a project or launch an enterprise may feel tedious, but it's worth it.

Reversed: Your occupation doesn't provide opportunities for improvement or advancement. You've mastered all the situation has to teach you, but your talents are underutilized. Low confidence, poor work habits or other factors may prevent you from realizing your potential. Alternatively, you may appreciate the situation's ease and stability, and conserve your energies for other areas. Whatever the case, pushing yourself a bit more would lead to greater material rewards.

NINE OF PENTACLES

Hands pluck flowers from a lush and beautiful garden, gathering them into a vase in the shape of a champagne flute. In the background, plump bunches of grapes hang from an arbor. This card suggests that your dreams have been realized. Relationships, both personal and professional, are stable and fruitful, and prosperity and abundance are yours. Savor it!

Reversed: Your life is stable and prosperous, but you are unable to relax and enjoy it. The work required to maintain your lifestyle may be too demanding, or your rise to affluence may have strained relationships or required compromises that leave you feeling isolated or guilty. Alternatively, leisure may simply bore you. Whatever the case, resist the urge to find fault, overindulge or self-sabotage.

TEN OF PENTACLES

A figure clothed in opulent robes sits among loved ones. The figure's hands are at rest, suggesting satisfaction and ease. The outstretched hands surrounding them each hold a gift that the figure has created and bestowed. This card concerns legacies and inheritances—those that benefit us and those we leave. It indicates that the success, wealth and status you achieve will lay the foundations for others' well-being. The traditions, stability and prosperity you help build will benefit your community for years to come.

Reversed: Negative legacies, such as traumas, debts or feuds, may be passed through generations, or traditions may become hollow or harmful. This card may also suggest the loss or reduction of an inheritance, or disputes over resources within a family or community.

PRINCESS OF PENTACLES

A woman gazes dreamily into the distance, lost in thought. Her hands and ears shine with jewels, and her serpentine hair reflects an earthy and sensual nature. This card may represent someone, usually feminine, who is eager for knowledge and experience. Often a student, apprentice or novice, this person is devoted to self-cultivation. She is warm, down-to-earth and loyal, and her confidence is inspiring. Though she has good practical sense, her idealism and naiveté may cause errors in judgement. This card may also suggest study, apprenticeship, training or a message that grounds you or brings you back to earth.

Reversed: An impractical person who drains energy and resources. Though intelligent, she focuses on material gratification rather than self-improvement, and she doesn't apply the attention necessary to develop her talents. This card may also indicate liberality, decadence, dilettantism, financial setbacks or bad news.

PRINCE OF PENTACLES

A young man looks up from his briefcase, pausing to consider his next move. With the seeds he carries, he knows he will sow an abundant crop, and visions of his harvest swirl around him. This card may represent an ambitious and intelligent person, usually masculine, with an entrepreneurial spirit. He is sensible and dependable, and will plug away at a task until he completes it to his own high standards. He knows he has much to offer and is eager to get started. This card may also represent a new job, a lucrative opportunity or success achieved through persistence.

Reversed: An apathetic and antisocial person who isn't fulfilling his potential. He may be unemployed or work a dead-end job that brings no joy. He may feel directionless and uninspired, but he isn't doing the introspection, research or networking necessary to discover his true calling. This card may also suggest inertia, stagnation or idleness.

QUEEN OF PENTACLES

A clear-eyed woman gazes approvingly at the blossoms and fruits that rise from her hands. With one palm, she supports the roots of a lush plant, and with the other, she sows new seeds. This card may represent a supportive, nurturing, cultured person, usually feminine, who is stable, grounded and calm. She is attuned to cycles of growth and understands the importance of sustainability and conservation. Her material and emotional security are rooted in careful management of resources, which she uses to cultivate a sustaining environment. This card may also refer to prosperity, generosity, sensuality, richness of spirit or reconnecting with nature.

Reversed: An overbearing and materialistic person who has difficulty making ends meet. Anxieties rooted in past scarcity may prevent her from appropriately managing resources in the present or planning for the future. This can lead to cycles of "feast or famine" that destabilize her environment and relationships. This card may also suggest discord, distrust, fear, greed or precarity.

KING OF PENTACLES

A proud and benevolent man stands among well-established trees and fruiting vines in a lush garden. His hands overflow with riches, and he offers them to you. This card may represent a powerful, influential and prosperous person, usually masculine. Though he has achieved material success, his priorities remain down-to-earth. He values his wealth only insofar as it brings joy and comfort to those he cares for. He seeks opportunities to invest in his community and to serve as a patron or benefactor. This card may also represent influencing others, living the good life, upholding tradition or benevolent conservatism.

Reversed: A successful and established person who may be prone to conspicuous consumption or extravagance—or, conversely, pennypinching. His mismanagement of resources damages relationships and disrupts and destabilizes his community. This card may also indicate money troubles, insecurity, or feeling possessive or undervalued.

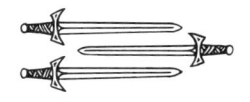

ACE OF SWORDS

Clouds part and a raised sword points out Polaris. Connections between constellations are visible, and the sword-bearer's knowledge has helped locate this lodestar. Confusion is over; a new direction is clear. This card indicates sudden clarity, a "Eureka!" moment or the start of a new way of thinking. A powerful new insight ends a period of mental conflict or indecision. You feel sharp and focused, and your intellect and analysis will be crucial in tackling whatever lies ahead.

Reversed: Your mind is clouded by self-defeating thoughts that masquerade as rational. You feel blocked, you overthink simple problems or you constantly second-guess yourself. This confusion prevents you from developing a clear direction. You may need to go with your gut.

TWO OF SWORDS

A handshake passes between crossed swords. An agreement has been struck, but both sides still grip their weapons. Tensions may be high, but an accord can be found. This card suggests that cooler heads will prevail. A conflict between opposing ideas or forces reaches a state of stability. This may be a stalemate, deadlock or cease-fire, but it is more likely an alliance or a meeting of the minds. Clear communication and impartial examination of both sides brings harmony.

Reversed: A balance of power has been disturbed, causing conflict and irrationality. Duplicity, cynicism or intellectual dishonesty may cloud judgement. Discord may be rooted in power imbalances, intellectual or otherwise. Confrontation may be required to restore stability.

THREE OF SWORDS

A heart is pierced by swords, and arrows fly from it in all directions. Storm clouds rain in the background, and blood drips down like tears. This card suggests that a relationship is disintegrating, and an agonizing separation, loss or breakup is underway. New knowledge may be to blame for your misery, and miscommunications or harsh words may cause further heartbreak. Differences cannot be reconciled; desires are incompatible. Have a good cry and let go.

Reversed: Heartbreak and loss overwhelm you. Disordered thinking drives you to isolation and rumination or causes you to lash out irrationally. While your situation is unfortunate and your feelings justified, negative thought patterns are making things worse. Don't salt your wounds; allow yourself to heal.

FOUR OF SWORDS

Three swords hang in brackets on a wall, while a fourth has been plunged into the earth. Roses grow on the last sword's hilt as the sun sets in the background. This card suggests that time for struggle has passed, and rest and recuperation are called for. A retreat, a vacation or simply a day off will help restore energies depleted by stress. Before making your next move, you may need to "sleep on it."

Reversed: You are unable or unwilling to take a time out to reflect on your situation. You may actively seek distraction, or you may simply have too much to do. Throwing yourself into work or getting overly involved in others' lives may be means to avoid being alone with your thoughts. Self-care and self-reflection are called for.

FIVE OF SWORDS

Two hands grip bundles of swords; two more hands hang severed and limp. Clouds close in, and raindrops drip down like blood. This card suggests that a major defeat, loss or humiliation has occurred. Your pride may be wounded, which may have played a role in your downfall. Alternatively, this card may represent a no-win situation or a "Pyrrhic victory." But devastating as it is, this loss has something to teach you.

Reversed: This card has roughly the same meanings reversed as upright, but the reversed position also indicates remorse, mourning and healing from the loss in question.

SIX OF SWORDS

A boat laden with swords navigates turbulent waters. The horizon it aims for is placid and starlit, and visions of flowers swirl around it. This card suggests that a journey is beginning. This may mean actual travel, or it may indicate gaining distance from a bad situation. You may get over something or leave something harmful behind. Whatever the case, this journey will take you to a better place.

Reversed: Your troubles cannot be easily escaped. Difficult disclosures or increased accountability may be necessary before you can move on. Alternatively, you may feel stuck, unable to imagine a better life or to leave an unhealthy situation. An external perspective may be helpful.

SEVEN OF SWORDS

A gloved figure sweeps five swords under a cloak, then disappears into the night. But two swords remain; the thief takes no more than they can carry. This card may suggest that accomplishing your goals in a hostile environment may require some sneaking around. Alternatively, you may be the victim of theft, betrayal or deceit. Either way, this situation is best approached with shrewdness, discretion and caution.

Reversed: Your prudence and integrity, while laudable, may be counterproductive. You may avoid taking risks or getting your hands dirty, or you may ignore pragmatic advice that strikes you as unsavory or cynical. This card may also suggest that a thief will be exposed or restitution given.

EIGHT OF SWORDS

A pair of bound hands struggles within a ring of swords. The swords are menacing, but they are also positioned to cut the binding cord if the captive makes the right move. This card indicates that you feel powerless and stuck. Your agency is undermined, and your hands feel tied. Muddled thinking, self-sabotage, and negative thought patterns compound this crisis, preventing you from recognizing how to free yourself. Nevertheless, there is a way out.

Reversed: You're breaking your chains, freeing yourself from thought patterns that held you back. You may be acting on instinct or emotion rather than logic, however, which could obscure certain dangers. Take care as you move forward.

NINE OF SWORDS

A pair of hands wring anxiously, menaced by a veil of swords. In the background, the full moon is eclipsed, the sky is dark, and raindrops fall like tears. But above it all stars are visible. This card suggests that you are plagued by guilt, shame, anxiety or regret. Your mind may race uncontrollably; unwanted thoughts or nightmares may keep you up at night. Your beliefs are self-destructive, and depression makes it difficult to see the way forward. But the situation may not be as dire as it seems. Don't lose hope.

Reversed: You may pull yourself from a state of depression or conversely, you may ignore or repress your negative feelings. Either way, facing fears and criticism is important at this time. Self-knowledge and self-acceptance are necessary to develop a healthier outlook.

TEN OF SWORDS

Two hands hang limp, punctured by swords. Blood drips from the wounds, and rain or tears pour down in the background. This card suggests that you're feeling defeated. Plans have come to naught, past achievements have been ruined and your ego has taken a major blow. The revelation of an error in your thinking may devastate you, and projects may lose meaning and worth. But don't surrender to negativity; things may look different in time.

Reversed: You begin to recover from what felt like a total loss. In the aftermath of a disaster, a bright side may reveal itself. You may feel strangely exhilarated or relieved; if the worst has already happened, you have nothing left to fear. Alternatively, you may feel cautious or anxious about a positive development, waiting on "pins and needles" for things to take a turn. Embrace this respite.

PRINCESS OF SWORDS

A young woman sits in a self-protective stance,

gripping a sword. Clouds swirl around her, revealing and concealing. This card may represent a sharp and quick-witted youth, usually feminine, who is on guard against falsehoods, manipulative rhetoric and faulty logic. She is a skeptic, and her criticism can be cutting. She has an answer for everything, but her assertions, though difficult to contest, may sometimes seem defensive, strategic or even cynical. This card could also represent a pessimist, an intellectually immature person, rumors, secrecy, guile or suspicion.

Reversed: This person is a contrarian who loves an argument and gets an ego boost from skewering others. She may be susceptible to paranoia or conspiratorial thinking, and her behavior likely stems from insecurities about her own intelligence. This card may also represent a lack of preparation, a lack of defense or an attack.

PRINCE OF SWORDS

A winged, but not quite angelic man gazes forward determinedly, gripping a sword. Lightning crackles from the blade tattooed on his chest, which he exposes for all to see. This card may represent a strong-willed and assertive individual—usually masculine, often with something to prove. He is intelligent and charismatic, but might also be a bit self-righteous or a know-it-all. He enjoys debate and his arguments are good, but impatience may prevent him from fully considering opposing views. This card may also indicate warnings, opposition, bravery or the aggressive pursuit of one's interests.

Reversed: A fanatic or ideologue who is quick to argue and apt to tilt at windmills. This person wields "rationality" as a weapon, but his logic seldom holds up to scrutiny. He may be vindictive, reverting to ad hominem attacks or other fallacies when his arguments fail to persuade. This card may also suggest vanity, nonsense, imprudence or ignorance.

QUEEN OF SWORDS

A woman raises a sword, cropping her own hair. Her eyes are clear, but haunted. Was her gesture an act of mourning or merely practical? Does her sword slice through the webs around her, or does it hang them? This card may represent an influential, intelligent, impassive person, usually feminine, whose aloofness allows a clear view of the complexity around her. She cuts through pretense to get to the heart of things, and her frankness can be intimidating. She may value high ideals or utilitarian logic more than individual relationships. This may make her seem cold, but there is wisdom in her calculations. Traditionally, this card was interpreted as a widow, divorcée or unmarried woman, but it may represent any independent person whose struggles have made them a less conventional thinker. This card may also represent privation, sorrow, abstraction or an intellectual crisis.

Reversed: A manipulative and deceitful person who deploys her deep knowledge of human behavior to influence others. She may mask her own intelligence so as not to arouse suspicion, or she may fail to fathom the true extent of her abilities and influence. Her duplicity and desire for control may stem from insecurities about her intelligence or attachments, rooted in trauma or loss. This card may also indicate hypocrisy, narrow-mindedness, intellectual manipulations or revenge.

KING OF SWORDS

A man in a suit stares over the rims of his glasses, a severe expression on his face. Though he carries a sword, he knows the pen is mightier and he has mastered both. This card may represent an intellectual or ethical authority figure who sets rules and distinguishes truth and falsehood. Though his power derives from rationality, intellect and expertise, he may exercise it in an authoritarian manner, expecting compliance without input. Like the Queen, he may be more faithful to ideals or abstractions than to relationships, but when your interests align, he can be a great ally. This card may also suggest a jurisprudence, mental fortitude or authoritarianism.

Reversed: A dictatorial, doctrinaire or ideologically rigid person in a position of power or authority. He is a harsh disciplinarian whose judgements may ignore nuance and whose punishments may not fit their crimes. This card may also represent being let down or poorly served by ostensibly rational institutions, such as the justice system, academia or government.

ACE OF WANDS

A hand descends from storm clouds, holding

a wand. At its lower end, the wand transforms into a pencil, ready to make its mark. At the upper end, it burns like a bush. Lightning flashes all around, and energetic arrows radiate from the place where the wand meets the earth. This card suggests that inspiration has struck, and its glory demands to be shared. Your mind is at its most inventive, and you are abuzz with fresh passions and transformative ideas. Creative sparks are flying, opportunities are emerging and new projects are taking shape. It's time to act!

Reversed: Factors critical for success are not present or not aligned, or you may not be in the right headspace. Projects undertaken now may suffer delays, setbacks or complications, and energy, passion and support may be hard to muster. The time is not ripe.

TWO OF WANDS

A serpent winds back and forth through a crossroads. Each path is planted with different flowers. The creature's head transforms to a raised hand; perhaps halting, perhaps blessing. Two wands are crossed before it. This card suggests that there are obstacles in your path. You are at a crossroads, but hesitate to take the next step. You may need time to assess the situation, consider your options or refine your vision for your journey. You may be afraid that you'll make the wrong decision or regret the path not taken. Whatever the case, do not linger too long.

Reversed: Stop to consider your decisions. You have a choice to make, but you shouldn't act rashly. The current situation is no longer working for you, and it may be tempting to take the first path out, but doing so may not bring the best results.

THREE OF WANDS

A ship sets sail under a compass rose. Its direction is true and its sails are full. This card suggests that strong foundations have been laid for future enterprises, and projects launched now will be successful. Your foresight and initiative are on the right track. Time and patience will be required to see results, but courage and bold action will be rewarded. This card could also indicate travel.

Reversed: Your efforts are stalling. You may feel stuck, unable to advance your goals or projects, or you may simply doubt that your efforts will produce rewards. Your plans may be impractical or overwhelming, or you may lack the resources to execute them. Simplifying your vision and managing expectations may help get you back on track.

FOUR OF WANDS

A banquet table laden with fruit and wine is garlanded with beautiful flowers. The sun is shining; all is well. This card suggests that you have much to celebrate. You've worked hard to achieve your desire; now is the time to relax and enjoy what you've created. This card may also suggest festivities marking life transitions, rites of passage or changes of season.

Reversed: The reversed card's meanings are similar to the upright; however, you may not feel as appreciative as you should, or you may feel ambivalent about your merits and accomplishments. Anxiety, insecurity or complacency may inhibit you from celebrating that which deserves to be honored. You have much to be proud of and to be grateful for!

FIVE OF WANDS

Hands struggle against each other in a flaming melee. The battle strips the wands they wield as weapons, leaving them leafless and barren. This card indicates that strife and conflict are present, and disagreements or power struggles disrupt your environment. Although competition can motivate and confrontations between opposing viewpoints can lead to greater insight, beware of conflicts fueled by grudges, jealousy, pride or greed.

Reversed: A dispute is nearing resolution, but may leave damage and hurt feelings in its wake. Third-party mediators, whether legal or otherwise, may need to get involved, and the results may ultimately feel more like a lose-lose than any kind of win.

SIX OF WANDS

Hands lift a laurel wreath, ready to crown a worthy victor. This card suggests that good news is coming. Your ambitions will be fulfilled, and your talents and achievements will be recognized. Accept your honors and be proud of what you've accomplished!

Reversed: Success may slip through your fingers or feel just out of reach. Arrogance or overconfidence may cause you to declare victory prematurely or dismiss inconvenient concerns that turn out to be important. Alternatively, you may get your hopes up about something that doesn't pan out. Either way, this setback is not final.

SEVEN OF WANDS

A raised fist thrusts up valiantly from a throng of wands and protest signs. Flames lick through the crowd, and the energy of the fist shakes loose leaves from the wand around it. This card suggests that it's time to take a stand. Don't be afraid to speak your mind or defend your position. Opposition can be overcome if you hold your ground and protect what you've gained. The effort may be exhausting, but the struggle is worthwhile.

Reversed: You may be unsure of yourself or where you stand. You may not be able to get a grip on a situation; perhaps you have trouble weighing all the factors or sorting through the complex histories involved. You may hesitate to judge or defer to those with more knowledge or conviction. Though this is likely the right approach, keep a critical eye.

EIGHT OF WANDS

Eight wands fly like arrows over a wall that has crumbled. Flowers sprout around it, and above, the sun shines through clouds. This card suggests that obstacles are falling away, and your goals can be achieved if you act with speed and focus. Seize opportunities as they arise, and don't linger over decisions or correspondences too long. This card may refer to "making a move"—romantically, professionally or otherwise—and to the accompanying rush of adrenaline. Energies are high, and conditions are in your favor, but they won't last forever. Take the plunge!

Reversed: The energy, initiative and inspiration you feel may be counterproductive. Your passion may be misdirected or obsessive, or your energies may be scattered or manic. Acting on these impulses will likely be disruptive, bringing more discord than joy or satisfaction.

NINE OF WANDS

Nine wands have been bound into a sturdy fence, and thorny flowers climb the timbers. Supported by this barrier, the plants have established themselves firmly enough to bloom, and their thorns defend against plucking. This card suggests that you've achieved a state of stability after many struggles and disruptions. Your experience may have made you guarded, but you've also gained wisdom, resilience and stronger boundaries. This prudence will serve you well, but defensiveness and self-isolation should be avoided.

Reversed: The walls you erect to protect yourself may do more harm than good. You may hold yourself back or construct self-imposed obstacles. Maintaining a strong front may feel safe, but letting yourself be vulnerable can lead to greater strength. Don't be afraid to let others in.

TEN OF WANDS

Two hands can barely hold the wands they carry. The blooming bundle is beautiful, but heavy. This card suggests that blessings may begin to feel like burdens. Success may bring responsibilities, challenges or complications you weren't prepared for. Confidence spurred by early wins may inspire you to fill your plate with projects that will ultimately exhaust you. Managing wealth or property may become difficult or stressful. Enlist the help you need, but don't forget to appreciate what you have.

Reversed: You may cling to obligations, situations or possessions that no longer serve you. Perhaps you carry others' baggage despite evidence that it isn't helping. Perhaps you take on more work than necessary when delegating would lead to better results. A project in which you've invested time, energy and resources may fail, but you may refuse to let go. Whatever the case, now is the time to lay down certain burdens.

PRINCESS OF WANDS

A young woman holds open a book, directing your attention to a relevant page. She is passionate about her subject and eager to share her knowledge. This card may represent a curious and intelligent person, usually feminine, who has information that may spark new ideas or cast problems in a different light. Avail yourself of her insight and expertise. This card may also represent doing research, giving advice, or getting excited about new ideas.

Reversed: A person who seeks to advise or inform you may instead cause confusion. Her information may be incorrect or just irrelevant—she may not have a full understanding of the situation. This card may also indicate ignorance, thoughtlessness, bad news, or a resistance to new ideas or inconvenient truths.

PRINCE OF WANDS

A young man straddles his motorcycle at the center of a deserted road. He's traveling alone, but his light shows the way forward. In his hand, he holds matches—one lit, and one extinguished. Will he set a fire, or simply light his cigarette? His eyes are hidden, and his dark glasses reflect only flames. This card may represent an adventurer and risk-taker, usually masculine, who follows his passions wherever they may lead. Irreverent, rebellious and innovative, he delights in upending the status quo. He has big ideas but doesn't sweat the details. Though his intentions are good, he may get more fired up by new interests than by long-term commitments. This card may also represent adventurous travel, unorthodox journeys, improvisation or going "off the beaten path."

Reversed: A reckless and foolhardy person who leaves others feeling burned. His passionate nature can make him temperamental or flighty, and he may be a "rebel without a cause." A thrill-seeker, he may be more attracted to the adrenaline rush of passion than to whatever he thinks he's passionate about. This card may also suggest relationship conflict, volatility or abandonment.

QUEEN OF WANDS

A woman holds a wand like a paintbrush or a pen, poised to create something new. The bolts of electricity in her hair show her crackling with energy, and the bubbles springing from her eyes show her overflowing with ideas. This card may represent a passionate, independent person, usually feminine, who radiates confidence, creativity and verve. She is a leader with a talent for inspiring others and transforming situations for the better. She is well connected and has energy and enthusiasm to invest. This card may also represent inspiration, determination, extroversion, theatricality or an enterprising spirit.

Reversed: A self-serving or volatile person who uses her intelligence and charisma to advance her ambitions and undermine those who oppose her. She may appear vengeful, petty or obsessive. This reputation is probably at least partly warranted, but her unwillingness to give in, give up or take abuse is also a source of strength. This card may also refer to deception, infidelity, politicking or interpersonal drama.

KING OF WANDS

A man with a mane of matted hair clutches a walking stick carved with a salamander. Like the salamander, he is not consumed by his inner fire; instead, he directs it. He walks his own path and transforms those he meets. His eyes may look wild, but they burn with the wisdom he's gained on his journey. This card may represent a powerful, honorable person, usually masculine, who may be an unorthodox teacher, an inspiring spiritual leader or disruptive entrepreneur. Though he values tradition, his genius and unique vision may result in behavior that others consider iconoclastic or eccentric. This card may also refer to integrity, maturity and courage.

Reversed: An arrogant, pretentious and autocratic person who resists others' input and makes rash or aggressive decisions. This person may cultivate an air of authority, expertise or originality that doesn't reflect their true abilities.

OPEN HAND TAROT SPREAD

An open hand bestows gifts, blessings, caution and more. The Open Hand Spread reveals insight into a situation and offers guidance going forward.

To begin, the querent shuffles the cards with a situation or question in mind. The reader may draw from the top of the deck after shuffling, or ask the querent to select individual cards from a fanned deck. Lay the cards face up in the order in which they are numbered here.

Depending on the type of guidance desired, Card 6 of this spread may be interpreted flexibly. Review the options on the next page and decide how you would like to interpret this card before beginning the reading.

CARD POSITIONS

1. SELF: Yourself in relation to the situation or question. What role you play.

2. CROSS: The situation that confronts you or the question you seek to answer. This card is upright when its top falls to the right.

3. HEAD: What you think about the situation or question. How you consciously or rationally understand it.

4. HEART: Your hopes, dreams, or desires (conscious or unconscious). What you'd like to attain.

5. BONE: Your fears or anxieties (conscious or unconscious). What you'd like to avoid.

6. LIMB: This card may be interpreted in one of three ways:
- Most likely outcome if the situation progresses along its current trajectory.
- Best possible outcome, given the nature of the situation and your outlook. This may not be the most likely outcome, and bringing it about may require concerted effort.
- Where you should direct your energies to satisfy the desires indicated by Card 4.

7. HAND: Next steps to help bring about the outcomes described in Card 6. If that outcome was not desirable, this card describes actions you'd want to avoid or resist.

ABOUT THE ARTIST

Liz Blackbird is an artist and writer based in the Midwest. Though largely self-taught, she studied visual arts at the Flint Institute of Arts in Michigan, the Maryland Institute College of Art, and the Ohio State University.

Liz was a contributor to *Pride Tarot: A Collaborative Deck*, published by U.S. Games Systems, Inc.

She can be reached at heartandhandstarot@gmail.com.

For our complete line of tarot decks, books, meditation cards, oracle sets, and other inspirational products please visit our website:
www.usgamesinc.com

Follow us on

Published by
U.S. GAMES SYSTEMS, INC.
179 Ludlow Street
Stamford, CT 06902 USA
www.usgamesinc.com